CU00922637

Create strategic collaborations.

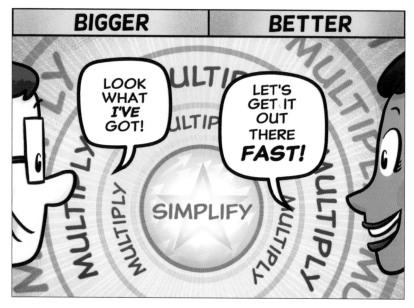

Simplifier-Multiplier Collaborations allow you to achieve breakthrough results while focusing only on what you do best and what comes most naturally to you.

Complexity's The Raw Material

First, You Simplify

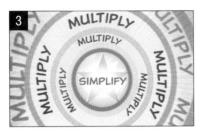

Then, You Multiply

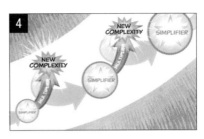

Simplify, Multiply, Repeat

Being One Or The Other

Being A 100% Simplifier

Being A 100% Multiplier

Collaboration That Always Does Both

Six Ways To Enjoy This Strategic Coach Book

Text **60 Minutes**	The length of our small books is based on the time in the air of a flight between Toronto and Chicago. Start reading as you take off and finish the book by the time you land. Just the right length for the 21st-century reader.
Cartoons **30 Minutes**	You can also gain a complete overview of the ideas in this book by looking at the cartoons and reading the captions. We find the cartoons have made our Strategic Coach concepts accessible to readers as young as eight years old.
Audio **120 Minutes**	The audio recording that accompanies this book is not just a recitation of the printed words but an in-depth commentary that expands each chapter's mindset into new dimensions. Download the audio at **strategiccoach.com/go/smcollaboration**
Video **30 Minutes**	Our video interviews about the concepts in the book deepen your understanding of the mindsets. If you combine text, cartoons, audio, and video, your understanding of the ideas will be 10x greater than you would gain from reading only. Watch the videos at **strategiccoach.com/go/smcollaboration**
Scorecard **10 Minutes**	Score your Simplifier-Multiplier Collaboration Mindset at **strategiccoach.com/go/smcollaboration**. First, score yourself on where you are now, and then fill in where you want to be a year from now.
ebook **1 Minute**	After absorbing the fundamental ideas of the Simplifier-Multiplier Collaboration concept, you can quickly and easily share them by sending the ebook version to as many other individuals as you desire. Direct them to **strategiccoach.com/go/smcollaboration**

Thanks to the Creative Team:

Adam Morrison

Kerri Morrison

Hamish MacDonald

Shannon Waller

Jennifer Bhatthal

Victor Lam

Margaux Yiu

Christine Nishino

Willard Bond

Peggy Lam

Simplifier-Multiplier Collaboration

Are you a Simplifier or a Multiplier? Every great entrepreneur is primarily one or the other, and identifying which you are adds deeper insight and meaning to the way you instinctively create value.

Once you know who you are, you can find the perfect collaborator: *your opposite*. Simplifier-Multiplier collaborations lead to unprecedented breakthroughs and results, and give you the freedom to focus exclusively on what you do best.

TM & © 2020. The Strategic Coach Inc. All rights reserved. No part of this work may be reproduced in any form, or by any means whatsoever, without written permission from The Strategic Coach Inc., except in the case of brief quotations embodied in critical articles and reviews.

Strategic Coach®, The Strategic Coach® Program, The Strategic Coach® Signature Program, Free Zone Frontier™, The Strategy Circle®, and The 10x Ambition Program™ are trademarks of The Strategic Coach Inc.

Cartoons by Hamish MacDonald.

Printed in Toronto, Canada. The Strategic Coach Inc., 33 Fraser Avenue, Suite 201, Toronto, Ontario, M6K 3J9.

This publication is meant to strengthen your common sense, not to substitute for it. It is also not a substitute for the advice of your doctor, lawyer, accountant, or any of your advisors, personal or professional.

If you would like further information about The Strategic Coach® Program or other Strategic Coach® services and products, please telephone 416.531.7399 or 1.800.387.3206.

Paperback: 978-1-64746-211-6
Ebook: 978-1-64746-166-9
Library of Congress Control Number: 2020903781

Contents

Introduction
Endless Complexity

You realize that you live in a world where everyone's complexity multiplies everyone else's complexity — and also that you have a solution.

Life radically changed in the early 1970s with the introduction of the microchip, followed by the personal computer, the internet, apps, and mobile communication.

These inventions have brought the economics, politics, and culture of the world down to the individual level. And individuals are asked more and more to use new technological capabilities to empower themselves to make sense of the world they're living in.

People say, "Isn't this great? We can do things faster, better, and cheaper." But what actually happens is that people get exponentially confused due to a lack of direction.

Everybody's reality, everywhere.
Everyone today lives in personal and public circumstances that are being disrupted in countless unpredictable ways that can make life complicated and confusing.

That was partially true 50 years ago, but it's a general condition now.

The essential culprit is that the complexity we each have can multiply the complexity everyone else has because we each have the interconnecting technology to complicate and confuse other people's lives.

So we're all complicit in the endless growth of complexity.

It's like we're fish, and complexity is now the water we swim in, and people think they can continue swimming the way they used to even though there's been a fundamental shift in our environment.

We haven't been trained for this interconnectivity and for this level of interaction that's required whether we like it or not.

So how does an individual not only survive, but thrive, in a new world without the protection of old structures?

You have to develop a whole new idea of what the individual has to focus on for themselves. That's half the picture. Then, you have to figure out whom to collaborate with— because the future is collaborative. And there are two fundamental skills of collaborating: *simplifying and multiplying*.

Complexity's a mindset.

While some people say that attention spans have gotten shorter, I think that attention spans have just become binary: you give 100 percent attention to things you're interested in, and zero percent to things you're not.

When you love doing something, that comes from the inside. And the complexity you experience isn't because of what's happening outside of you, but rather because of how you're thinking about your relationship to the outside world.

You have no responsibility for what's happening in the outside world, but you have 100 percent responsibility for how you respond to it.

You can't play a 50/50 game, feeling like you have some control over what's happening outside of you and not taking full ownership of your response to what's happening.

It used to be that we had access to limited resources, but we're now able to connect with any resource or capability we want, so we have to take responsibility for figuring out what resources and capabilities we should be looking for.

Mindsets that work for you.
If you took someone from 200 years ago and put them into the world 150 years ago, they'd be overwhelmed by the advances in technology that were present.

But the rate of change has accelerated in our time. And the question is, can you adjust your mindset to the current set of conditions?

The secret to life at all times is to develop mindsets that adjust to the circumstances you're living in and give you access to the best possible resources and capabilities for your own personal growth.

That would be true anywhere, in any time period.

But there's a dependency now on guidance from outside sources, and that isn't working anymore. Traditional teachers, leaders, and guides don't know any more than you do about what will be required of you years in the future.

Skills for best thinking.
So what we do is continually create, test, refine, and strengthen entire systems of useful mindsets that increasingly enable us to be successful in a world with other like-minded individuals. We look for resonance.

We continually organize, package, and share uniquely new and useful ways of thinking about the world that also enable other like-minded individuals to think and act in better ways.

So once you've proven it with yourself, you become valuable to others. We find guidance in our relationships with like-minded people.

Simplicity for everyone.
Things have gotten more complicated for everyone. Complexity is the water we're swimming in, and to an extent, there's no air to breathe outside of that water.

You don't need to spend time explaining the problem because it's the experience we're all living in. And not everyone has learned how to swim in this ocean of complexity yet.

To know who you are in this world and to have great, mutually beneficial relationships with other people, you have to become increasingly skillful at transforming your own internal complexity into new ways of simplifying everyone else's internal ability to transform their complexity.

If you want simplicity, this is how to get it.

Chapter 1
Complexity's The Raw Material

You recognize that everything becoming more complex is your greatest opportunity for creative collaboration.

Decades ago, people didn't have to deal with the amount of complexity we have in our lives right now.

But in this way, things are actually far simpler than they used to be because everybody in the world has the same problem. We're totally unified and equal in this way.

So let's look at what everybody thinks is the problem—and then switch it around to see that it's actually the key to the solution.

Complexity is good.

You can commit yourself to looking at the complexity in your daily life as something endlessly good that you can transform into uniquely useful resources and capabilities for yourself and others.

Every day, there's a certain amount of complexity available to me that I haven't handled yet. There are new elements and new challenges, and interactions are different. What's required of me in the here and now keeps changing.

But I've made the decision that all of the complexity in my life is mine. I'm going to take 100 percent ownership of it.

I know that by completely owning my complexity, I'll come up with solutions—ones that are useful beyond me.

Creativity protects you.

As soon as you begin making complexity more useful, you'll understand that this creative process protects you from all of the negative impacts of complexity that confuse, paralyze, and overwhelm others.

It has to start with each individual taking 100 percent ownership of their own complexity. Think of the instructions on airplanes that you should always secure your own oxygen mask in cases of emergency before you help anyone else with theirs. Likewise, if a process you've come up with to solve a problem hasn't worked for you, you won't be in a position to use it to help anyone else.

Something that I've found as I've become more creative in transforming my own complexity is that other people's problems with complexity are just none of my business unless I can do something about it.

Endless opportunity.

The process of successfully transforming complexity into new forms of value will get more powerful the more you do it. As a result, you'll feel more confident, calm, and capable as time goes on.

The key is to stop being resentful of the complexity—and to stop resisting it. This will open up your creative abilities, which will lead you to being useful and to being protected from the negative impacts of complexity.

I think of complexity as my friend. And being able to say this is a major dimension to cross into. I want to stay interested and challenged, and complexity is always what's given me the best new raw material to work with.

Every day, there's a chance to start over with new things. There will be more than enough for you to work on, so there's no reason to set highly unrealistic goals like simplifying all of the complexity in the world. You'll have plenty of your own, and you can consider it a success if you solve even part of that.

Welcoming the waves.

The ever-increasing waves of new complexity created by other people are a wonderfully abundant thing you'll come to welcome, as your greater success at transforming it each day makes you more valuable to yourself and others. When you wake up every day, you have the chance to become yet more valuable.

A lot of people give themselves a hard time, and then they export that to others, but it won't be like that for you. You'll recognize the complexity that's being generated by everyone as a good thing, an endless wave of opportunity, and so you'll never be hard on yourself or on anyone else about this situation of endless complexity.

This is a new attitude for dealing with something that keeps getting bigger, more complicated, more complex, and more confusing: not only are you okay with it, you actually love it.

Because I've adopted this stance and attitude, I've found that as things in the outside world seem to be speeding up more and more, things are actually slowing down for me in a pleasant and predictable way.

And while you might have heard it said that you shouldn't make your life just about you, you also can't make your life about others unless you start with yourself.

You can't focus on trying to solve other people's complexity and ignore the complexity in your own life. If something didn't work on you, you have no credibility to try it out on someone else.

I want to be useful, but not to every single person. I want to be useful and create value for the right audience, and I want that usefulness to grow every quarter. That's all I can do.

Solving others' confusion.

The secret to always making the growing complexity of the world into a positive experience lies in using your growing knowledge and skills to bring about new and amazing solutions to the worst problems of complexity that others experience.

You'll develop a growing storehouse of what seems to always work, what seems to never work, and everything in between, so you'll never be starting from scratch when it comes to being useful to other people.

It's paying attention to and taking ownership of your own experiences that will help you learn and discern, always adding to that storehouse of knowledge and strategies.

Chapter 2
First, You Simplify

You continually solve problems for yourself and then for others by transforming complicated situations into simple breakthroughs.

It takes patience to approach simplifying complexity in the best possible way.

When something's not entirely clear, you don't want to act in a way or say something that will make it even less clear. Showing frustration or irritation doesn't help; it only makes you part of the problem. And you don't want to add anything to what's not working.

You can't always solve something right away. It requires patience and tenacity. Sometimes, a lot of waiting is involved. You might have to try a few things before you come upon the solution.

Simplify now, easier tomorrow.

Every day, I'm faced with a lot of complexity. Here's my rule for choosing what to start with: I pick the easiest thing to simplify today that will make my life less confusing and complicated tomorrow.

For example, I've noticed that my health and fitness go a little bit off track if there's a morning where I don't weigh myself. When I do weigh myself in the morning, a game plan immediately emerges in my mind so that tomorrow, my weight won't be any higher.

If a way you have of doing something works, don't stop doing it. Once it's simple, don't make it complicated. It works for you, and it works for you uniquely.

We all have to start with our own experiences because when something works for someone, it's because they've custom designed it for themselves.

Your idea may provide only 80 percent of the value for other people, but you have to figure out the other 20 percent to actually make it work completely for yourself. No person's direction or advice can provide 100 percent of the required usefulness to anyone else.

When you give someone advice or make a suggestion based on what works for you, you have to allow the other person to say, "I'll take only the portion of this that's useful to me."

Everyone has their own unique goals, and there's a lot going on with each individual, so we have to let other people develop their own unique solutions.

Proof of one success.

After your first simplifying success with one complexity, the confidence that comes will promptly motivate you to simplify a second thing, then a third, and so on. And as you move along, it's important to recognize what works and what doesn't.

Every morning, I write down five things I'm proud of that I haven't previously given myself credit for. Then I think of and write down five things that haven't worked—these could be things that didn't work yesterday, or things that aren't working on an ongoing basis.

Finally, I come up with and write down five improvements I can make today. Doing this keeps things running. And if I've made it through the list of five improvements by 3 p.m., I start a new one.

But it's about more than whether I actually do everything; it's the fact that these things are consciously registering every day. Be a friend to yourself, not a taskmaster. Give yourself nudges—don't beat yourself up.

You'll find that as you're more careful and alert about yourself, that will extend to how you deal with other people. It will help you determine how to present something so that it's useful instead of adding to someone's complexity.

Easier and faster.

Just as the experience of growing complexity in your life had seemed endless and hopeless, you'll discover that this process of simplifying one thing after another, day after day, becomes easier and faster.

If, previously, the world was running your life, you're now reversing that force. You're in charge.

Since complexity is a factor for everybody, you'll find points of simplification in a variety of areas—if it seems like everyone is doing things a certain way, or using a certain product, it might be that there are simplifying benefits or some other kind of usefulness there.

So appreciate the simplifications that already exist and bring those in as you move forward with handling your unique daily complexities.

Clearer and calmer.

Each new simplification you make will bring clarity and calm, whereas previously, the experience of growing complexity made you feel more anxious and overwhelmed. When you start in this new direction, you'll feel alone, but it won't take you a year to get a handle on this. It just takes doing it several days in a row.

It involves adopting the mindsets that we've covered here and accepting responsibility for your own complexity, believing that it's good and can be used as raw material, and that if you simplify complexity, you'll be useful to others. In addition to bringing clarity and calm, simplifying complexities in your life will give you a sense of control.

One, ten, a hundred.

Being the simplifier of your own complexity will give you greater capability and confidence, and you'll want to share with others how they can simplify their own lives.

People will pick up on the change in you before you even tell them about it. You'll seem less rushed, less busy, and better able to concentrate. Others will want to gain the personal momentum you have, and you'll naturally want to share it.

There won't be any negative self-comparison involved; with these mindsets, each person is always moving forward with simplifying their complexity, only comparing their own todays with their own yesterdays.

And yet, as you focus on your own knowledge, you'll become more attuned to and more useful to others than you were before.

Chapter 3
Then, You Multiply
You continually increase your personal
and business success by multiplying your
usefulness to everyone who matters most.

Multipliers multiply usefulness. But you can't multiply your
usefulness for everybody. You might have a great resource,
but time, attention, and energy are limited, and you want
to make the most of them. So, you have to be more
discriminating about whom you're useful to.

The best multiplier to simplify.
When you look at the marketplace, you'll find millions of
examples of people taking complex things and simplifying
them. These simplifications can show up as products,
services, processes, bypasses, replacements, and so on.

Consumers want things that make life faster, easier,
cheaper, bigger, better, more convenient, and more
comfortable. And for any existing product or service out
in the world, there is someone who can look at it and say,
"I think there's a simpler, easier way of doing this."

Simplifying can involve putting two things together to create a third, or taking something that already exists and
adding something to it, and the result is a better solution
than anything that's already out there.

The best way to increase your productivity and profitabil-
ity is to take your most valuable simplifier—where you've
simplified something complicated and others have found

it valuable—and *multiply* its value out in the world in the fastest possible ways. So, first, it has to be proven as being valuable to others, and then it becomes a matter of scaling.

Who gets helped most.
The easiest way to identify your best simplifier is to determine which of your offerings most helps the individuals who mean the most to you.

An example from my own life and business is The Strategy Circle, the Strategic Coach tool at the foundation of a lot of what we do.

I had gone through the process of one-on-one coaching maybe 80 to 100 times before I realized that no matter the specifics of an individual's goals, the process was largely the same. And after creating The Strategy Circle to work from, I got faster at asking the right questions, and the whole coaching process became simpler and easier.

Something to remember is that your simplifier or your multiplier is worthless until you get positive feedback from a check writer. And it's when the individuals being helped mean the most to you, when they're the people you want to be a hero to, that it's time to look at multiplying the number of those individuals that your solution is helping. That's how you grow it.

How you already do it.
Everyone loves getting a desired result in a simpler, easier, faster way, and we've all been adopting such simplifiers since we were children. Time is precious, and we grade a process or tool's value in terms of whether it allows us to get something done in a simpler way.

The process of simplifying and multiplying is human. There's a natural desire that, if we get a result with a certain amount of effort now, we'd like to get that same result—or bigger—with less effort in the future.

Our bodies work like this too. When we do the same exercise routine on the third day, we expect it to take less effort than it did on the first day.

You can multiply your current best simplifier just by looking at the successful ways you've already multiplied your best simplifiers in the past. Even if you're primarily a Simplifier, as a successful entrepreneur, you've already multiplied, so you know how to do it. Whether you packaged your sales process and trained other salespeople on it, or replicated a great store design and opened another location, multiplying simplicities has been your success formula as you've grown your business.

New exponential technologies.

You'll become increasingly confident about your multiplying success in the future because new skilled individuals will continually support your best simplifiers—and your biggest multipliers—with new exponential technologies.

We live in a world where multiplying is getting easier and easier. The technologies that are getting developed and released are totally supportive to us as individuals wanting to make our desired impacts in the fastest ways possible while minimizing complication and complexity.

If you're a Simplifier and you want to multiply the usefulness of a simplifying process, you don't necessarily need to learn how to use the technology that will get you there. You just need to work with people who can perform that multiplication for you. Team up with a Multiplier to make it an easier, more enjoyable process, letting them use their expertise to multiply your simplifier.

Many collaborators can help.

As soon as you create a new, better simplifier that others find valuable, many new kinds of Multiplier collaborators will emerge to help you increase your new value creation. You know this from your past successes.

At Strategic Coach, our associate coaches multiply our impact. This year, we'll put on 500 workshops, and I'll coach only 44 of those myself. Compare that to 1995, before we collaborated with our first associate coach, when I coached 136 workshops myself.

I'm now freed up from doing nearly 70 percent of that work, and this is because the associate coaches multiply us out in the world. Plus, we're making use of all sorts of technology, putting out podcasts and books that support people's experience, multiplying our impact.

Collaboration is key to all of this working for you, and you have to know what your role is or things will get complicated.

If you're a successful entrepreneur, you've had experience in both simplifying and multiplying. But you can now choose which one you want to focus on and stay 100 percent on that side of the line, knowing that just on the other side is someone who can do the other part of the process and focus 100 percent on that.

Chapter 4
Simplify, Multiply, Repeat

You are completely clear that all future progress in a complex world requires combining simplifying and multiplying.

There are almost eight billion people in the world, and most of them have cell phones and access to the internet, so simplifying and multiplying is happening all the time and its reach is very, very far.

Part of the reason you have to simplify and multiply is that an increasing number of other people are doing this, and complexity is coming as a result of the impact of it. You have to operate by taking this reality into account.

Things are different than they were 50 years ago, and you can't operate in the world the way people did back then and expect things to still work.

We've crossed a boundary into a new way of approaching our experiences, and you need to be alert, curious, and responsive to your own experience. In a changing world, having a handle on your own experience—knowing what you like and what you don't, whom you like working with and whom you don't, making decisions based on these factors, and simplifying your life—is a constant good that will last for your entire lifetime.

Completely clear formula.
Your past achievements and successes show that your new progress in our increasingly complex world has to be

based on constantly simplifying and multiplying, creating new value.

In the past, it was most likely just you doing everything that was needed, both the simplifying and the multiplying. But now you've broken it down into two distinct categories: making something *better* through simplifying, and then making it *bigger* through multiplying. You simplify complexity, and then you multiply the simplifier.

Every time you do this, you add to the complexity of the people who had previously solved the issue you're now simplifying, but that's not your problem. They themselves also need to go about simplifying and multiplying.

All truly successful people have learned how to simplify and multiply consciously. The question now is whether each person is primarily a Simplifier or a Multiplier.

How complexity seems to work.
You can see now that instead of being a worrisome problem as it once seemed, complexity is actually pointing to a wonderful, permanent solution. Complexity will work for you if you start working with complexity.

It's created by all of the simplifiers and multipliers, and it provides the raw material for you to create a new simplifier. Then, you take the simplifier out and multiply it, which puts some more complexity out into the world for the people who used to provide the solution you just replaced with your simplifier.

Combining two capabilities.
You have activities available to you right now that are either simplifiers or multipliers, which when you combine them in

new ways, will immediately move you forward faster and more easily.

You'll improve your business by asking yourself questions like, "What can be made simpler?" and "What needs to be multiplied?"

Until you recognize that you're primarily either a Simplifier or a Multiplier, every opportunity will be attractive to you, whether it's suited to you or not and whether it's worth pursuing or not.

It's not necessary that you do both activities, simplifying and multiplying, yourself, though both are necessary. What's important is that you focus on what you're best at and team up with someone who's great at what you're not.

Progress always requires both.
Our education system tends to instill in us that every individual needs to be good at everything, and that each of us needs to have all the skills necessary for projects to be successful. But that just isn't true.

There are a lot of people in the world, and so if you're a Simplifier, you can count on being able to find someone else to do the multiplying, and if you're a Multiplier, you can be sure there are Simplifiers out there who need you to make their simplifiers bigger.

You can focus only on simplifying or only on multiplying as long as you recognize that the one you don't do is still essential. It's the other part of the equation.

Trying to make your life exclusively about either simplifying or multiplying without the other never gets you very far.

Progress in every area of life only happens when Simplifiers and Multipliers are working together.

Can't fight it, so use it.

Much if not all of your individual and organizational failure and frustration before now has come from trying to ignore, escape from, or fight back against complexity.

This is silly when you think about it, since the trick to overcoming complexity is simply to combine your best simplifiers with your best multipliers.

If you review your past successes and failures, you'll likely find that when things didn't work, you were acting as both the Simplifier and the Multiplier without realizing the significance of either role. You were just doing everything that needed to be done, but you had no notion of the distinction between the activities.

There have probably been times when you were simplifying when you should have been multiplying, and multiplying when you should have been simplifying, because you didn't really know the difference.

The problem was that you were dealing with issues of complexity, but you didn't have a way of approaching complexity like you do now.

Complexity is way bigger than you. It can't be stopped or controlled. And you don't need to stop it or control it. You just need to have a way of working with it.

Chapter 5
Being One Or The Other

You now accept that the best collaboration in every situation is between a skilled Simplifier and a skilled Multiplier.

In every best collaboration, each of the capabilities involved—simplifying and multiplying—is in the hands of an individual who is particularly skilled at that capability and has totally committed themselves to that part of the collaboration.

When you're completely comfortable and confident with your collaborator taking care of the other capability, it allows you to focus just on what you're doing and are best at. You don't have to worry about what they're doing or how they're approaching their part of the project. There's total trust.

If you don't have total confidence in your collaborator, you'll have competitive thoughts about how they *should* be going about performing their part of the collaboration. Even if it's not your area of skill, you'll be thinking about and judging how they're going about things, second-guessing what they're doing.

You have to be 100 percent committed to *either* simplifying or multiplying. If you're only 95 percent committed, you'll be five percent thinking about the part of the collaboration you're not responsible for.

Always knowing who you are.

Your best strategy going forward, in relation to every kind of complex situation, is to decide right now if you're a

Simplifier or a Multiplier. Do you simplify complex problems or do you exponentially multiply others' innovations?

Whichever you are, you'll start stockpiling individuals who have the other capability with whom you can collaborate.

As long as you know what your strength is, what your capability is, you'll know what else needs to be involved in a collaboration in order for it to be the most successful it can be.

Your success in a complex world.
Everything's changing regarding what being "successful" means.

It used to be that there were mediations between us and the complex world, but now, every individual has a direct electronic relationship with the complexity of the world. Now, success is entirely about continuous, never-ending, skillful collaboration between you and others.

Success means that you're making bigger and better improvements that are valuable to others and satisfying to yourself. It means that you can't think of anything you'd rather be doing than what you're doing.

This is because this Simplifier-plus-Multiplier equation doesn't remove 50 percent of the complexity from any situation. It removes about 95 percent right off the bat. And it enormously reduces the amount of competition in your life.

You can take comfort in knowing that once you're committed to either simplifying or multiplying, the success you have in collaborating with others will be continuous. You'll always be able to reduce complications and competition, and you'll always be able to create the biggest, best, most satisfying value.

Best possible collaborations.

Now that you're focusing on it, you'll get more and more proof that the best collaborations you've ever experienced and observed are those between great Simplifiers and equally great Multipliers.

You'll also be able to see why there are tensions in some business partnerships, when one person or the other hasn't fully committed to their capability. If you're doing 100 percent of your capability but you aren't sure that the individual you're collaborating with will do 100 percent of theirs, that's a problem.

A great example of a Simplifier-Multiplier collaboration is between Apple's Steve Jobs (Multiplier) and Steve Wozniak (Simplifier). Where would one be without the other? The benefit of these types of collaborations is that both people's talents and skills are necessary to bring ideas to life and create major breakthroughs.

Consciously, skillfully dedicated.

Regardless of what trial and error, failures and successes, you've experienced up until now, the way forward comes from consciously dedicating all of your skills to being one or the other of two kinds of collaborators. Doing this will both simplify and multiply your future opportunities, achievements, and successes.

I've noticed that ever since I determined that I'm a Simplifier, all of my work has taken a jump because I'm focused only on simplifying things. I respect that that's my only role in collaborations.

I recognize that multiplying is always a problem that will need to be solved, but it won't be my problem to solve.

I'm always alert, curious, responsive, and resourceful about potential collaborators and technologies I can partner up with to do the multiplying while I do the simplifying.

The more you test out situations, the better sense you'll have of which ones work best, and you'll reach a point where you'll be able to say, "If I do my part 100 percent, I totally trust that the other 100 percent capability will show up, and I can't make any judgments about the quality of the other capability, because that capability isn't my thing." And the success of the collaborations will be evident in the results.

New solution, new rules.

As soon as you recognize that you're either a Simplifier or a Multiplier, your immediately obvious collaborations will start to create entirely new solutions in the marketplace, establishing new rules for achieving individual and organizational success.

The real value of what your collaborations produce, what you and your collaborators bring to the table, will be determined by what benefit they have for your target audience.

You'll see the value you've created and feel the satisfaction that comes with that whenever you introduce something to the marketplace that helps people capture their opportunities, eliminate their dangers, and maximize their strengths.

ARE YOU A SIMPLIFIER?

Chapter 6
Being A 100% Simplifier

You know you're a permanently dedicated Simplifier if that's always your first thought in any new situation.

When you're totally confident about what you do, and you're clear about which capability you have—simplifying or multiplying—you'll find that your mind automatically goes to how you can apply that capability and get that part of the job done.

And you never have the stress of having to do 100 percent of the problem solving, because if you're a Simplifier, you don't even need to think about the multiplying half of the equation.

How you always start.

If you're a Simplifier, then you know from reviewing how you approach any kind of complex situation or circumstance that you always start taking action in the same way: simplifying things in your own mind.

You do that before you do anything else.

How it works for me is that I go into my mind and recognize that there's a lot going on in the situation at hand. Then, I determine what the center of the issue is. With the approach that no new idea is bad, I go about simplifying.

Very first thought.

My very first thought is always, "Where's the center of this, which, if I find it, will let me ignore everything else?"

Simplifiers have a well developed and systematic way of thinking about anything complicated and confusing, and it starts off with asking that question.

A complicated and confusing situation is complicated and confusing to everyone. It's usually something new, and no one's prepared for it.

But say there are ten factors that seem to make up a complicated situation. What I do is see if it can be enormously simplified by figuring out if one of the ten factors should be focused on first. If so, then nine of them can be completely ignored for now.

Once you're clear about where the center is, you know where to start. And that simplifies everything.

Multipliers will go straight to asking themselves, "Who's the first person I should take this to?" but as a Simplifier, what you do is go for the essential factor that determines the usefulness of the situation itself.

Being a Simplifier myself, I'm passionate about finding the center of complicated situations. I never get tired of that activity, and every time I do it, it feels like a fresh start, something totally new.

Permanent simplifier.
If you're a 100 percent, permanent Simplifier, anytime you're required to do something that doesn't start with simplifying, it won't excite you or hold your interest.

Once you're committed to it, you go all the way to 100 percent simplification. And that's the only way to be a great collaborator.

Knowing that your collaborator will take care of 100 percent of the multiplying is why you'll never have to think about or worry about how that part will get done. Total dedication and commitment from everyone involved is part of the formula for success.

Complicated things clear.

Being a Simplifier from now on means that you'll always be increasingly valued and rewarded for making complicated situations—complexity that confuses people and causes conflict—clear in the fastest possible way.

Imagine the value you provide from everyone else's point of view: a skilled, dedicated Simplifier can look at a situation that's puzzled people and say, "This might seem overwhelming, but here's how it really is. We start by focusing on this one factor."

You recognize that complexity isn't a bad thing but rather the raw material you use in order to find solutions and move forward. That's how you create simplifications quickly while other people are paralyzed, not knowing what to do.

And as a reward for doing what you do best, your skill will be utilized and appreciated, your capability will get enhanced, you'll get referred and gain a reputation for your value, and your status will grow.

Collaborating with Multipliers.

You can now be increasingly choosy about all of the future situations you engage in because you'll only want to be involved in those where you can make the greatest improvements—and that can only happen by collaborating with individuals who are 100 percent Multipliers.

You can expect to get the quality of collaborators that you want because you're putting as much in as you expect to get on the other side. Dedication attracts dedication, commitment attracts commitment, and confidence attracts confidence.

So you might as well go in 100 percent for being a Simplifier, because that's the level you want in a Multiplier you collaborate with.

But you have to be in the pool yourself before you call out for someone else to join you. And you have to be 100 percent a Simplifier to make sure you never enter into competition with a Multiplier, your collaborator. You want to stay completely on your side and for them to stay completely on their side.

If you're only 50 percent a Simplifier, you're not going to attract a 100 percent Multiplier because you'll seem complicated to them.

But being a 100 percent Simplifier, you won't offer any opinion on how the Multiplier does their part other than praise.

Why would you spend any of your time thinking about the capability that someone else does better than you, other than to be thankful that the other person is doing it? That's the freedom of Simplifier-Multiplier collaboration.

Chapter 7
Being A 100% Multiplier
You know you're a totally dedicated Multiplier if enlarging and expanding new simplifiers is what you most love doing.

Simplifiers can get frustrated by having a great idea that they don't know how to get out into the world.

As the Multiplier, you see the Simplifier's great idea and envision what you can do and what connections can be made in order to maximize the impact and opportunity of the idea.

You don't feel a need to be involved with the creation of the idea or to ask the Simplifier to modify the idea in any way. Just taking the simplifier capability and making it useful to others gives you joy.

When you try to be the Simplifier yourself, it's hard work that leaves you frustrated and fatigued, just like when a Simplifier tries to multiply things.

What you always do.
If you look back at how you approach any kind of complex situation, you'll realize that you always start by taking others' best simplifiers and multiplying their usefulness outward into the world.

A Simplifier always goes inward, looking for the center of things, and a Multiplier always goes outward, expanding the simplifier's value and reach.

Doing one of these activities is always one's natural instinct, and if you try to do the other, you're literally working against yourself. A Multiplier trying to simplify can get paralyzed for years.

There's some humility that's required here; you have to acknowledge, "This half is what I'm good at, so my job only exists on this side of the line."

And while you and the Simplifiers you collaborate with have different capabilities, what you have in common is who you want to be a hero to.

Multiplier strategies and systems.

As a Multiplier, you have well-developed and systematic strategies and processes that answer this question: "Who are the best existing users who can most quickly benefit from this new simplifier?"

The Simplifiers have already done their job, so the issue now is who would benefit the most from what they've created, and who would use it the fastest? Your point of view is: "Great idea. How does it become a great result out in the world? How does this move things forward?"

Maybe you haven't always been paid enough for doing this in the past, but it's such a great experience for you that there are times when you'd probably do it for nothing.

And while this quality isn't particular to entrepreneurs, entrepreneurs have the most freedom to run with ideas that they know will have a big result.

They don't need to ask permission before acting on it.

Other Multipliers' networks.

You not only use new simplifiers to benefit your own users, you also introduce them to other Multipliers like you who will enthusiastically introduce the new simplifier to the users in their networks who will most benefit from its value.

You stockpile Simplifiers because the process always has to start with them, but you also stockpile Multipliers so you can get ideas out there really fast.

So the best Multipliers—those who are truly into collaboration—make deals with each other; they don't compete with each other. And that's one way great Multipliers grow: linking up with other great Multipliers.

Increasingly alert and responsive.

As you have more and more success in multiplying new simplifiers through growing networks, you'll become more and more alert about and responsive to even better new simplifiers that can expand your growing Multiplier success.

The rewards for your successful multiplying will expand too. Simplifying and multiplying are two complete, and different, universes, but understanding and having access to the universe of simplifying will be a big part of your growing success, even though you're a Multiplier.

You really have to pay attention to the Simplifier universe so you can spot a great new idea right away and jump on getting it out into the world. Once you've gone through the process, you know what you're looking for, and with more experience, you won't waste any time or effort.

Collaborating with Simplifiers.

Everything will work—in even better and more surprising ways—for your endless multiplying success as long as you keep increasing your ability to collaborate with those innovators who keep providing you with even better new simplifiers for your Multiplier networks.

You don't make it hard for Simplifiers to take advantage of your Multiplier capabilities. You make it very easy, and you make it attractive.

And you don't fool around with the simplification they've created. You take it as they've done it, and you multiply that out in the world.

But once you've had enough experience, you can inform them that you've multiplied a lot of simplifiers, and you can tell them what things will be like for their simplifier out in the world.

That's how Simplifiers learn to improve on their side of the line. They want what they do to get multiplied out in the world, so they need to know and take into account the rules when it comes to multiplying.

And you tell them, from your experience, what the simplifier they've created needs to look like and how it needs to be packaged in order to be successfully multiplied.

So the best collaborations include people on both sides of the line staying in their lane, but also communicating and adjusting according to the other's expertise.

Chapter 8
Collaboration That Always Does Both
You continually grow your future 100x every time you're inside of a 100% Simplifier and 100% Multiplier collaboration.

When you and your collaborator come together, you bring 100 percent of your capability, and you expect your collaborator to bring 100 percent of the other capability. You both have the highest of standards for each other.

It isn't a 50/50 split, where each person is seeking a missing piece to complete the whole. If you did only 50 percent of your capability, you'd be 50 percent paying attention to the other side of things, thinking about what your collaborator is doing and how you might do it differently.

In the best collaborations, two wholes come together, and there's no chance of any competition between you because you're each doing something completely different and unique.

Everything is collaboration.
Every next opportunity for improvement you see will automatically become a 100x collaboration opportunity because you'll immediately see it entirely in terms of combining two "100 percents"—yours and someone else's.

Since I'm a Simplifier, every time I come up with a new idea, I automatically check it through all of the Multipliers I work with and figure out who my collaborators should be.

I know that I don't have the multiplying skills that they have, so the line is clear in my mind, and my only focus is to do the best I can on my side of the line.

These 100 percent collaborations allow me to do only what I do best—the simplifying. Once I reach the line that separates simplifying and multiplying, I know the rest is not my job. That's where someone else brings in their 100 percent capability.

First time is forever.

As soon as you've tried it once, and experienced how extraordinarily easier, faster, and more enjoyable it is, you'll know forever that Simplifier-Multiplier collaboration is the only way to grow in every area of your life.

Once you've tried the easy way, why would you ever want to go back and do it the hard way? Your past experience wasn't a waste of time, though, because you now know what you don't like in a collaboration.

And even now that you have the blueprint for Simplifier-Multiplier collaborations, you might still not get the results you're looking for, or you might find that the process of the collaboration isn't as easy or as enjoyable for you as it should be.

In those cases, you have to figure out if it's you or your collaborator that's the problem. Not every Simplifier is a right fit for every Multiplier.

What your brain looks for.

By the time you're inside your first successful 100x collaboration, your suddenly transformed "100 percent brain" won't be looking for anything else. Going forward,

Simplifier-Multiplier collaborations will be the only capabilities that matter.

For the rest of your life, success is going to be about putting your 100 percent in collaboration with other people's 100 percent.

This simple formula of 100% Simplifier plus 100% Multiplier will always overcome complexity and bring the best results.

The collaborations you engage in are a new capability. On your own, it's like performing manual labor. But when you combine your 100 percent with another person's 100 percent, you suddenly have access to electricity. You go from candles to hydro.

You can now recognize that when something in the world really works, there's a combination of Simplifier and Multiplier capabilities going on, whether that's apparent from the surface or not.

And when something's successful over a long period of time, it must be that the collaborators know where the line is between their capabilities and consciously reproduce their success.

Opportunity everywhere.
Until you identified which 100 percent you are, you could never really see true collaboration possibilities. But now that you're completely clear, you'll see everyone and everything in terms of Simplifiers and Multipliers.

You'll see in all your past experiences where you got energy and where you were frustrated and fatigued by what you were doing.

When you had a painful experience, what was the activity? You were probably doing something that wasn't your natural instinct, and so it was doomed to be a negative experience from the start.

Now that you recognize that you're either 100 percent a Simplifier or 100 percent a Multiplier, and you give up 100 percent responsibility for the other capability, you'll be amazed by how much you can get done week after week without feeling like you're putting in a lot of effort.

The clarity you have now lets you know exactly what you're looking for moving forward so you can get big results easily and enjoyably, never crossing your side of the line.

Nothing else is needed.

Once you begin your lifetime Simplifier-Multiplier collaboration journey, nothing else is needed to increasingly grow 100x in every area of your personal and business life. It all lies in your capability, and in your recognizing the capability you need someone else to do.

Other factors, like technology, can only help if you stay on your side of the line. If you're a Simplifier, technology can further simplify what you're doing, and if you're a Multiplier, technologies can exponentially expand your multiplication.

But if you're a Simplifier trying to multiply, or vice versa, technology and other tools are only going to exponentially multiply your frustration.

Tools are useful only if they support your doing what you do best.

Conclusion
Complexity And Collaboration Future
Your growing Simplifier-Multiplier collaborations continually take advantage of the endless new complexity created by "Complicators."

Both Simplifiers and Multipliers work on transforming complexity—but who's supplying the complexity?

People who aren't Simplifiers or Multipliers.

Complexity never ends because every simplification and multiplication causes complexity for the things that suddenly don't work anymore.

The simplification that gets multiplied out in the world is an improvement—faster, easier, more effective—on whatever already exists, so every Simplifier-Multiplier collaboration results in new complexity for the people who aren't engaging in those collaborations.

Those who don't collaborate.
Everyone in the world who's neither a Simplifier nor a Multiplier is a "Complicator"—someone whose efforts to succeed only produce new complexity, confusion, and complications.

Complicators tend to always blame someone else for things not working. Complaint is part of the complexity of the world.

If you don't know who you are in terms of how you create value in the world, it complicates all the areas of your life.

Everything's connected. If things are really working, that can be expanded through other things that work, and if things really aren't working, that multiplies as well.

You have to know who you are and respect that. Because it's also true that if you're a Simplifier who crosses the line into Multiplier territory or vice versa, you're a Complicator.

If you know the secret but disobey the rules, you're not being true to yourself, and all you'll produce is frustration.

When someone knows they're a Simplifier or a Multiplier but does the other capability anyway, it's usually because they're going for status. Status is the fastest way to forget the rules.

Just remember what you're good at and what other people find valuable in you. And no matter how much success you have, don't forget the collaboration formula that got you there.

Complicators can't collaborate.

As a 100% Simplifier or a 100% Multiplier, you can recognize that every Complicator in the world will have to go through the same transformation process that you have in order to escape from their frustrating complexity.

There's no place for a Complicator in a Simplifier-Multiplier collaboration. Every individual in our endlessly complex world has to choose to be 100 percent one or the other before they can collaborate.

If a Complicator does identify as a Simplifier or Multiplier but they're not 100 percent committed to it, they'll still be engaging in competition with whomever they try to collaborate with, and it won't be a relief for their complexity.

Your collaborations show the way.

The single best thing you can always be doing for yourself and the people who matter most to you is to continually create and expand entirely new value in your world through Simplifier-Multiplier collaborations.

In the past, you've probably worried about performing a necessary capability that isn't yours, but you don't have to do that now that you understand that you're a 100% Simplifier *or* Multiplier and that you'll always be able to find someone to collaborate with who has the other capability.

Whichever side of Simplifier-Multiplier collaborations you excel at, keep doing that and it will keep creating new value. Others will be inspired by this to do the same.

The ability to focus on what you're great at without worrying about what the other side is doing isn't just twice as good, but exponentially better and more efficient.

This is because if you're thinking about the other side, you have no insight into how it should be getting done, but you still have judgments about how you could do it better. But you couldn't.

Recognizing your side of the line and staying on it involves humility and respecting your own uniqueness. There's a golden rule here: Treat your collaborators uniquely, letting them do their part in their own way, and they'll grant you the same respect. There's trust in collaboration, just as there's mistrust in competition.

Collaboration attracts and transforms.

As soon as you begin succeeding as a 100x Collaborator, others who are also collaboration-minded will quickly transform themselves to join your new and better way forward. And it doesn't have to be a long, laborious process; they can do this very quickly by identifying whether they're a Simplifier or a Multiplier.

Everybody wants what you have—easier and faster success. So when other people see you in action and want that for themselves, you can tell them what you're doing differently.

You can tell them that they have to do only the activities and tasks that they enjoy and to give up what's bad and difficult for them. It might be a challenge for those who have defined their life as being difficult, but still, even the most frustrating people have the desire for things not to be frustrating.

And the more people you inspire to identify as either a 100% Simplifier or a 100% Multiplier, the more people you have to potentially collaborate with.

Everyone is uniquely responsible.

For the rest of your life, you're responsible only for your own unique Simplifier-Multiplier collaborations. Creating your own uniquely surprising new kinds of collaborative value in the world is all that you'll ever need to concern yourself with.

Everyone else can make the same choice—to be unique.

And there's never been a better time to make that choice.

The Strategic Coach Program
For Ambitious, Collaborative Entrepreneurs
You commit to growing upward through three transformative levels, giving yourself 25 years to exponentially improve every aspect of your work and life.

"Simplifier-Multiplier Collaboration" is a crucial capability and a natural result of everything we coach in The Strategic Coach Program, a quarterly workshop experience for successful entrepreneurs who are committed and devoted to business and industry transformation for the long-term, for 25 years and beyond.

The Program has a destination for all participants—creating more and more of what we call "Free Zone Frontiers." This means taking advantage of your own unique capabilities, the unique capabilities around you, your unique opportunities, and your unique circumstances, and putting the emphasis on creating a life that is free of competition.

Most entrepreneurs grow up in a system where they think competition is the name of the game. The general way of looking at the world is that the natural state of affairs is competition, and collaboration is an anomaly.

Free Zone Frontier
The Free Zone Frontier is a whole new level of entrepreneurship that many people don't even know is possible. But once you start putting the framework in place, new

possibilities open up for you. You create zones that are purely about collaboration. You start recognizing that collaboration is the natural state, and competition is the anomaly. It makes you look at things totally differently.

Strategic Coach has continually created concepts and thinking tools that allow entrepreneurs to more and more see their future in terms of Free Zones that have no competition.

Three levels of entrepreneurial growth.
Strategic Coach participants continually transform how they think, make decisions, communicate, and take action based on their use of dozens of unique entrepreneurial mindsets we've developed. The Program has been refined through decades of entrepreneurial testing and is the most concentrated, massive discovery process in the world created solely for transformative entrepreneurs who want to create new Free Zones.

Over the years, we've observed that our clients' development happens in levels of mastery. And so, we've organized the Program into three levels of participation, each of which involves two different types of transformation:

The Signature Level. The first level is devoted to your *personal* transformation, which has to do with how you're spending your time as an entrepreneur as well as how you're taking advantage of your personal freedom outside of business that your entrepreneurial success affords you. Focusing on improving yourself on a personal level before you move on to making significant changes in other aspects of your life and business is key because you have to simplify before you can multiply.

The second aspect of the Signature Level is how you look at your *teamwork*. This means seeing that your future consists of teamwork with others whose unique capabilities complement your own, leading to bigger and better goals that constantly get achieved at a measurably higher rate.

The 10x Ambition Level. Once you feel confident about your own personal transformation and have access to ever-expanding teamwork, you can think much bigger in terms of your *company*. An idea that at one time would have seemed scary and even impossible—growing your business 10x—is no longer a wild dream but a result of the systematic expansion of the teamwork model you've established. And because you're stable in the center, you won't get thrown off balance by exponential growth. Your life stays balanced and integrated even as things grow around you.

And that's when you're in a position to transform your relationship with your *market*. This is when your company has a huge impact on the marketplace that competitors can't even understand because they're not going through this transformative structure or thinking in terms of 25 years as you are. Thinking in terms of 25 years gives you an expansive sense of freedom and the ability to have big picture goals.

The Free Zone Frontier Level. Once you've mastered the first four areas of transformation, you're at the point where your company is self-managing and self-multiplying, which means that your time can now be totally freed up. At this stage, competitors become collaborators and it becomes all about your *industry*. You can consider everything you've created as a single capability you can now match up with another company's to create collaborations that go way beyond 10x.

And, finally, it becomes *global*. You immediately see that there are possibilities of going global—it's just a matter of combining your capabilities with those of others to create something exponentially bigger than you could ever have achieved on your own.

Global collaborative community.

Entrepreneurism can be a lonely activity. You have goals that the people you grew up with don't understand. Your family might not comprehend you at all and don't know why you keep wanting to expand, why you want to take new risks, why you want to jump to the next level. And so it becomes proportionately more important as you gain your own individual mastery that you're in a community of thousands of individuals who are on exactly the same journey.

In The Strategic Coach Program, you benefit from not only your own continual individual mastery but from the constant expansion of support from and collaboration with a growing global community of extraordinarily liberated entrepreneurs who will increasingly share with you their deep wisdom and creative breakthroughs as innovators in hundreds of different industries and markets.

If you've reached a jumping off point in your entrepreneurial career where you're beyond ready to multiply all of your capabilities and opportunities into a 10x more creative and productive formula that keeps getting simpler and more satisfying, we're ready for you.

For more information and to register for The Strategic Coach Program, call 416.531.7399 or 1.800.387.3206, or visit us online at *strategiccoach.com*.

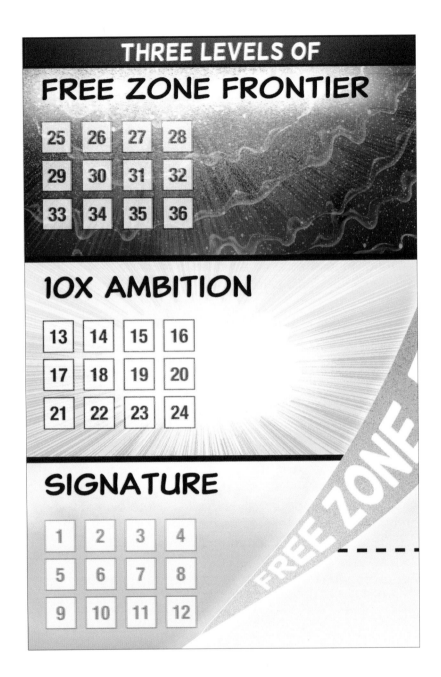

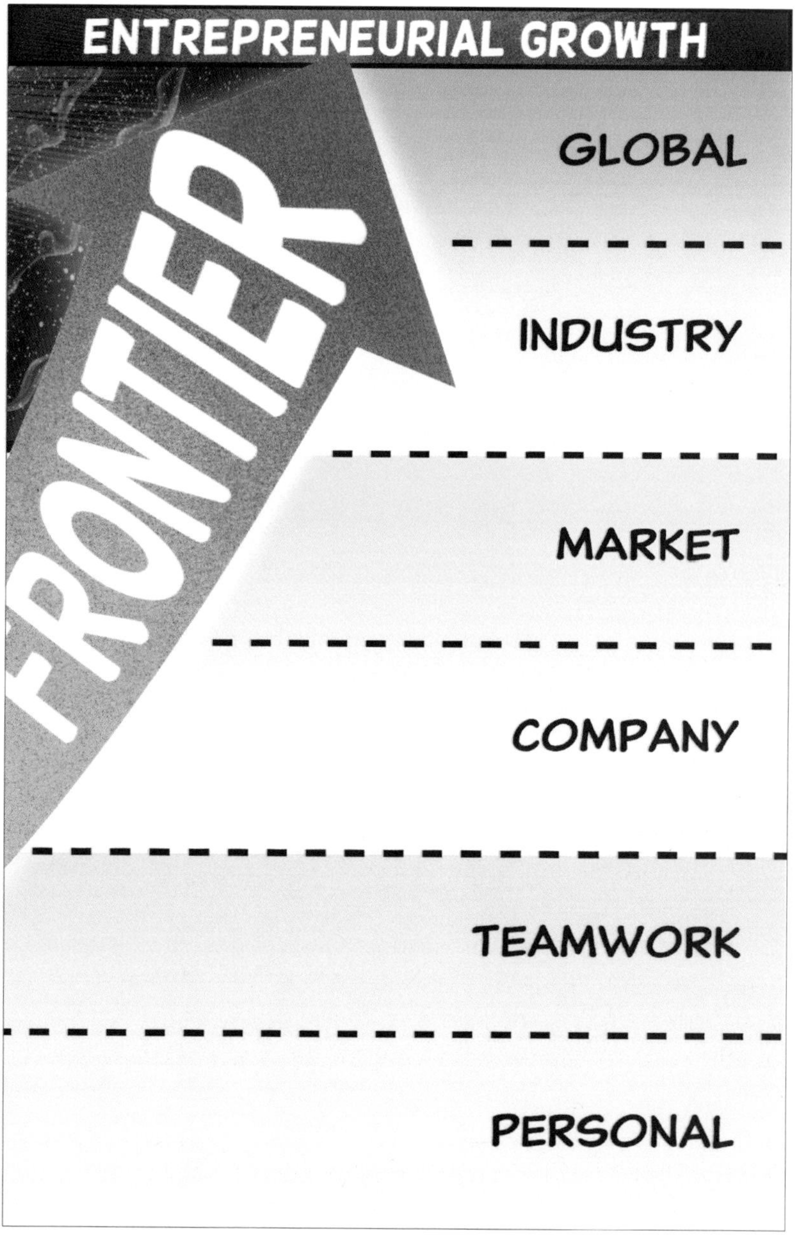

ENTREPRENEURIAL GROWTH

FRONTIER

GLOBAL

INDUSTRY

MARKET

COMPANY

TEAMWORK

PERSONAL

Simplifier-Multiplier Collaboration Scorecard

Turn the page to view the Mindset Scorecard and read through the four statements for each mindset. Give yourself a score of 1 to 12 based on where your own mindset falls on the spectrum. Put each mindset's score in the first column at the right, and then add up all eight and put the total at the bottom.

Then, think about what scores would represent progress for you over the next quarter. Write these in the second scoring column, add them up, and write in the total.

When you compare the two scores, you can see where you want to go in terms of your achievements and ambitions.

Mindsets	1	2	3	4	5	6
1 **Complexity's** **The Raw Material**	You are so overwhelmed by the complexity of today's world that you've given up trying to understand how to deal with it.			You are so frustrated and fatigued by growing complexity that you're willing to transform your entire mindset.		
2 **First, You** **Simplify**	You've never had the ability to deal with the complexity of your own life, and therefore are not useful to others.			You've reached a point, both personally and professionally, where you have to simplify everything in your life.		
3 **Then, You** **Multiply**	You seem to be capable only of multiplying your complications and confusion, making you less aware of outside change.			You are tired of trying to expand your success on your own, and now you want to find new ways to multiply yourself.		
4 **Simplify,** **Multiply, Repeat**	You've never learned how to simplify or multiply because learning anything new and useful is always too difficult.			You're just starting to see how the most successful achievers you know have made progress by simplifying and multiplying.		
5 **Being One** **Or The Other**	You never know who you are in relation to any kind of confusion or complication, and never know where to start.			You're suddenly aware that you haven't been successful because you've never been either a Simplifier or a Multiplier.		
6 **Being A** **100% Simplifier**	You've never been a dedicated anything in your life, so you don't have any experience of creating simple solutions.			You're starting to understand that all of your future success is going to come from making complicated things simpler.		
7 **Being A** **100% Multiplier**	You're one of those individuals who has never figured how to grow anything in your life nor would you even know how to begin.			You are increasingly aware that most of your past failure is directly the result of not multiplying others' simplifiers.		
8 **Collaboration That** **Always Does Both**	You've never known what you are, which also means that you never know how to collaborate with anyone else.			You've failed every other way to be personally successful, and now you're 100% ready to try the collaboration route.		
Scorecard	➡	➡	➡	➡	➡	➡

7	8	9	10	11	12	Score Now	Score Next
You've established a stable occupation and lifestyle where your status protects you from other people's complexity.			You recognize that everything becoming more complex is your greatest opportunity for creative collaboration.				
You've always become more successful by following other people's best solutions without creating any of your own.			You continually solve problems for yourself and then for others by transforming complicated situations into simple breakthroughs.				
You've always hitched the success of your career and life to the momentum of more successful achievers.			You continually increase your personal and business success by multiplying your usefulness to everyone who matters most.				
You have reached a point in your successful life where you're confident that everything can stay the same.			You are completely clear that all future progress in a complex world requires combining simplifying and multiplying.				
Your success and current status in life have come from following other people's successful examples and rules.			You now accept that the best collaboration in every situation is between a skilled Simplifier and a skilled Multiplier.				
Your life is modeled on best practices of the most successful people who have greater status than you've earned so far.			You know you're a permanently dedicated Simplifier if that's always your first thought in any new situation.				
You've always had good sense about hooking yourself to other people's growth through no ideas or talent of your own.			You know you're a totally dedicated Multiplier if enlarging and expanding new simplifiers is what you most love doing.				
You've gotten where you are simply by following the rules that more successful people have mastered and taught you.			You continually grow your future 100x every time you are inside of a 100% Simplifier and 100% Multiplier collaboration.				

About The Author
Dan Sullivan

Dan Sullivan is the founder and president of The Strategic Coach Inc. and creator of The Strategic Coach® Program, which helps accomplished entrepreneurs reach new heights of success and happiness. He has over 40 years of experience as a strategic planner and coach to entrepreneurial individuals and groups. He is author of over 30 publications, including *The 80% Approach*™, *The Dan Sullivan Question*, *Ambition Scorecard*, *Wanting What You Want*, *The 4 C's Formula*, *The 25-Year Framework*, *The Game Changer*, *The 10x Mind Expander*, *The Mindset Scorecard*, *The Self-Managing Company*, *Procrastination Priority*, *The Gap And The Gain*, *The ABC Breakthrough*, *Extraordinary Impact Filter*, *Capableism*, *My Plan For Living To 156*, *WhoNotHow*, *Your Life As A Strategy Circle*, *Who Do You Want To Be A Hero To?*, *Free Zone Frontier*, and *Always Be The Buyer*, and is co-author with Catherine Nomura of *The Laws of Lifetime Growth*.

Printed in Great Britain
by Amazon

17662764R00047